FROM INTROVERT TO EXTROVERT

A GUIDE TO EMBRACING YOUR TRUE SELF

BY

DAVID I. WOOD

opinion. While every effort has

been made to ensure the accuracy

of the information presented in this

book, the publisher and the author

assume no responsibility for errors

or omissions.

Contents

INTRODUCTION

If you're an introvert, do you ever feel as though you're losing out on life because you're not as outgoing as your extroverted friends? Do you believe that your lack of the same social abilities as your extroverted classmates is keeping you from reaching your full potential? If so, you are not by yourself. Many introverts suffer with feelings of not belonging or not reaching their full potential.

But, the fact is that introverts are just as capable as extroverts. Simply said, introverts communicate in various ways. In contrast to extroverts, introverts are often more reflective and contemplative. They frequently find it challenging to be in big groups or to engage in small chat, preferring instead to spend their time alone or with a select number of close friends.

The good news is that introverts may discover methods to express themselves that seem natural and comfortable and can learn to love who they really are. To accept their genuine self and make the most of their introverted nature, introverts should follow these advices:

1. Embrace your introversion. Don't try to be something you're not. Instead, accept and embrace your introverted nature.

2. Find your own way of expressing yourself. Introverts often have a unique

way of expressing themselves, so find what works for you and don't be afraid to be yourself.

3. Spend time alone. Introverts often need time alone to recharge and process their thoughts and feelings. Make sure to take time for yourself and do things that make you feel relaxed and happy.

4. Connect with others. Introverts don't have to be completely isolated. Find ways to connect with others that feel comfortable and authentic to you.

5. Take risks. Don't be afraid to take risks and try new things. You may surprise yourself with what you can do.

By embracing your true self and finding ways to express yourself authentically, you can make the most of your introverted nature and live a fulfilling life.

CHAPTER 1

Understanding Introversion and Extroversion

In psychology, extroversion and introversion are two of the most often used words. They refer to two different personality types, and realizing how they differ might make it easier for you to comprehend both yourself and other people. The definitions, traits, and potential effects of introversion and extroversion on interpersonal interactions will all be covered in this article.

INTROVERSION?

Focusing on one's own interior sensations, emotions, and ideas is a sign of introversion. Most introverts are more reticent and prefer to be alone themselves or with a small group of close pals. They often take pleasure in reflective and contemplative pursuits including reading, writing, and music listening.

Reading, writing, and other solitary pursuits are popular hobbies among introverts. An introvert is likely to prefer spending time alone themselves and find time with big groups of people less rewarding. Introversion has also been characterized by some as a preference for a peaceful, less exciting external environment. Introverts are quickly overwhelmed by too much stimulus from social events and involvement. Often seen in growing toddlers and teenagers, they prefer to focus on one task at a time and prefer to observe circumstances before they join. Prior to speaking, they are more contemplative.

The average introvert is introverted, reflective, and reserved and often finds it challenging to fit in with others. The introverted personality is also characterized by excessive daydreaming and contemplation, thorough weighing of factors before making judgments, and withdrawing under pressure. In contrast, the extravert exhibits traits like extroversion, receptivity to other people, activity, aggression, and the capacity for fast decision-making.

It's easy to mistake introversion for timidity. Shyness results from discomfort, whereas introversion is preferred. Although not necessarily fearing social interactions as shy individuals do, introverts like solitary over sociable pursuits.

EXTROVERSION?

Extroversion is a personality trait characterized by a focus on external activities and interactions. Extroverts tend to be more outgoing and enjoy spending time with large groups of people. They often enjoy activities that involve socializing, such as attending parties, going out to eat, and participating in team sports.

Being with other people gives extraverts energy and makes them thrive. Large social gatherings, such as those at parties, community events, political rallies, and business meetings, are enjoyable to them. They frequently do well in groups.

An extraverted individual will probably prefer spending time with others and feel fewer fulfillments in solitude. When they are with other people, they tend to be more energized, and when they are alone, they are more likely to become bored.

Behavior of an Introvert/extrovert

Extraverts and introverts vary in a variety of ways from one another in terms of their behavioral traits. One research found that introverts like functional, comfortable clothing whereas extraverts tend to wear more ornamental attire. Compared to introverts, extraverts are more inclined to like peppy, mainstream, and dynamic music. Personality also has an impact on how individuals set up their workspaces. Extraverts tend to have more elaborate workplaces, leave their doors open, have additional seats close by, and are more likely to place candy bowls on their workstations. These are efforts to get coworkers together and promote conversation. Contrarily, introverts prefer to decorate less and set up their workspaces in a way that discourages social engagement.

Notwithstanding these differences, a meta-analysis of 15 experience sampling studies found that the behaviors of extraverts and introverts had a lot in common. In these researches, participants utilized mobile devices to record several instances from throughout their everyday lives in which they acted extraverted (e.g., brave, outspoken, forceful, outgoing). Fleeson and Gallagher

(2009) discovered that extraverts and introverts often exhibit extraverted and introverted behaviors, respectively. In fact, there was greater intra-individual than inter-individual variation in extraverted behaviors. The main difference between extraverts and introverts was that the former tended to behave moderately extraverted 5–10% more often than the latter. According to this viewpoint, extraverts and introverts are not "fundamentally different". The idea that extraversion is more about what one "does" than what one "has" suggests that a "extravert" is just someone who behaves extraverted more often.

Since introversion-extraversion ranges along a continuum and because people are varied and unique, they may exhibit traits from both orientations. People may learn to behave in "contra dispositional" ways in certain settings, such that someone who acts introverted in one circumstance may act extraverted in another. Individuals have the capacity to adopt "free characteristics," acting in ways that may not come naturally to them, but which strategically promote goals that are significant to them. All of this paints a positive picture of extraversion. Individuals' extraverted behaviors fluctuate depending on the situation, rather than being constant and unchanging. They might also choose to be extraverted to further key personal goals or simply to feel happier.

Some Behavior of an Introvert

A person who is more preoccupied with their inner world than their surroundings is said to be an introvert. They are more likely to be reserved, quiet, and reflective. They often choose to be alone themselves or with a select group of close pals. Also, they could be more susceptible to extrinsic cues like loud sounds and crowded areas.

Introverts often take more time to assimilate information and are more introspective and deliberate. They could take longer to join discussions or answer to inquiries. Also, they can be more inclined to watch and listen than to speak out.

Moreover, introverts may think independently and with greater creativity. They could be more prone to look outside the box and develop original solutions to issues. They could also be more inclined to take their time and carefully weigh all of their alternatives before choosing.

Moreover, introverts may be more sensitive to criticism and take longer to bounce back from failures. They could be more inclined to internalize their sentiments and more prone to depressive or lonely feelings.

Moreover, perfectionists and procrastinators may be more common among introverts. They could also be more susceptible to feeling overburdened by an excessive amount of work or knowledge.

They exhibit timidity as well and may avoid social settings more often. Also, they could feel uneasy in huge crowds or strange environments more often.

Behavior of an Extrovert

A person who is extroverted, chatty, and socially inclined is an extrovert. They often seek out social settings and are known for being the life of the party. Being near other people gives them energy, and they often love conversing and exchanging ideas.

Extroverts are sometimes seen as the life of the party since they frequently start discussions and entertaining events. They are often seen as the fun-loving, extroverted, and gregarious people who are always ready for an adventure.

Extroverts often communicate their thoughts and emotions more honestly and openly. They often feel more at ease speaking about their thoughts and emotions than introverts do. Also, they are more willing to experiment and take chances.

Extroverts are sometimes the most outgoing and sociable people, and they are frequently the ones that are always up for a good time. Often, they are the ones to start talks and other activities. They are often seen as the fun-loving, extroverted, and gregarious people who are always ready for an adventure.

Extroverts often communicate their thoughts and emotions more honestly and openly. They often feel more at ease speaking about their thoughts and emotions than introverts do. Also, they are more willing to experiment and take chances.

Compared to introverts, extroverts are often more extroverted and gregarious. They often start discussions and organize events, earning them the reputation of being the life of the party. They are often more comfortable talking about their thoughts and experiences than introverts are, and they are frequently more open and expressive with their sentiments and emotions. Also, they are more willing to experiment and take chances.

However they may also be serious and contemplative, extroverts are often seen as chatty and extroverted. They often exhibit more openness to new experiences and greater risk-taking tendencies. They often feel more at ease in social settings and are more inclined to start discussions and activities.

Introvert-extrovert personality differences in relation to the following areas.

SOCIABILITY

Extrovert and introvert types behave quite differently in social settings. Whereas introverts are often quiet and introverted in social circumstances and frequently prefer to avoid social situations completely, extroverts have a propensity for seeking out, participating in, and enjoying social interactions.

Extroverts are more socially active, thrive on the energy of people around them, and often find themselves the center of attention in big social gatherings. Introverts are typically quieter and love spending time alone.

This is not to argue that introverts are antisocial; rather, they enjoy their lives more when they are not subjected to the overstimulating environment that social gatherings provide.

COMMUNICATION

The propensity of extroverts to speak more often and loudly, to occupy more physical space by making bigger gestures, and to start more conversations than introverts is the root of their high social presence. Extroverts made more eye contact and talked more often during interactions with an unknown individual than introverts, according to a small survey of undergraduates.

Also, extroverts perceive nonverbal communication far more confidently and accurately than introverts do.

DECISION-MAKING

Introverts are more prone than extroverts to utilize early information to develop judgments and make choices in time-constrained circumstances. According to studies on how extroversion and introversion affect decision-making, extroverts tend to act more quickly and on what seems most natural at the time. While it was shown that extroverts exhibited quality-checking behavior before making selections, they still need guidance when presented with crucial choices.

In contrast, introverts rely mostly on their own judgment, intuition, and deliberate thinking to avoid making rash judgments.

Extraverts often have more favorable opinions of life in general and their careers are no different in the workplace. Positive correlations between extraversion and professional satisfaction have been shown in the research. Extroverts are also more inclined than their introvert counterparts to act to improve bad job conditions.

Introverts experience noise disruptions in the workplace more than extraverts do. Although extroverts purposefully chose greater noise levels, noise distraction severely hindered the ability of introverts to concentrate.

INTERESTING FACTS

Whereas extroverts discover their "true me" via more conventional social encounters, introverts are more likely to find their "actual me" (the core of who they really are) online. The significance of communicating the "true self" calling it a vital life skill. Those who struggle to communicate their "true self" are more likely to have severe psychological problems. It is believed that social networking sites like Facebook and Twitter provide introverted people a way to meet new people.

Those who spend a lot of time on social media (more than two hours per day) see them as being more extroverted and outgoing.

Several forms of job training have distinct effects on introverts and extroverts. A comparison of ideation skills training (which focuses on idea development) with relaxation training, according to extroversion levels, focusing on opening the mind and removing mental barriers). Although ideation skill training is more successful for extroverts, the training is especially advantageous for introverts.

Extroverts are more prone to want instant gratification and to be susceptible to impulsive, incentive-driven behaviors.

They are also more inclined to engage in risky activities like as extreme sports.

Introverts and extroverts communicate in quite different ways verbally. Introverts are more prone to concentrate on tangible details whereas extroverts often use more abstract language.

CHAPTER 2

Exploring Your True Self

Discovering and being aware of your actual self is a process. Understanding who you are, what you want, and how to live a life that is authentic to you is all part of this path. Discovering your true self and figuring out how to live in accordance with your values and beliefs are both steps in this process.

To discover your actual self, you must first become conscious of your thoughts, emotions, and actions. This entails taking the time to pause, observe, and think about your attitudes, emotions, and actions. Knowing that your ideas, emotions, and actions don't always reflect who you really are requires you to be honest with yourself.

Finding your basic values and beliefs is the next stage. This requires considering your values and the things you hold dear. Being honest with you is crucial, as is accepting the possibility that your values and views have evolved through time.

The next stage is to investigate how your basic values and beliefs are manifested in your life once you have recognized them. This entails taking a close look at your decision-making processes, interpersonal interactions, and time management. Recognizing that your principles and ideals may not always be represented in your behavior and being honest with yourself are vital.

Taking action is the last stage towards discovering your actual self. Making adjustments to your life that are consistent with your values and beliefs falls under this category. Being honest with you is crucial, as is realizing that change might be challenging and take some time.

Discovering who you really are takes time and effort. It's crucial to have patience and understand that finding your real self and living in accordance with your principles and beliefs may take some time. It's also critical to remember to treat one well and to continuously be developing and learning.

EXPLORING YOUR TRUE SELF AS AN INTROVERT

Exploring your true self as an introvert and finding happiness can be a difficult journey. It requires a lot of self-reflection and introspection. Here are some tips to help you on your journey:

1. Take time to be alone: As an introvert, it is important to take time to be alone and reflect on your thoughts and feelings. This can help you gain clarity and insight into who you are and what makes you happy.

2. Connect with nature: Nature can be a great source of solace and peace for introverts. Taking a walk in the park or going for a hike can help you clear your mind and reconnect with yourself.

3. Practice mindfulness: Mindfulness is a great way to become more aware of your thoughts and feelings. It can help you gain insight into what makes you happy and what doesn't.

4. Journal: Writing down your thoughts and feelings can be a great way to explore your true self. It can help you gain clarity and insight into who you are and what makes you happy.

5. Spend time with people who understand you: Surrounding yourself with people who understand and accept you can be a great way to explore your true self. It can help you feel more comfortable and confident in whom you are.

6. Take risks: Taking risks can help you gain insight into who you are and what makes you happy. It can also help you become more confident in yourself and your decisions.

7. Find your passion: Finding something that you are passionate about can be a great way to explore your true self and find happiness. It can help you feel more fulfilled and connected to yourself.

It might be challenging to discover your actual self as an introvert and achieve pleasure, but it is doable. You may learn more about whom you are and what makes you happy by spending time alone, getting outside, practicing mindfulness, writing, hanging out with people who get you, taking chances, and pursuing your passions.

Finding your passion is essential to understanding who you are as an introvert. It is crucial to take the time to think about your passions and how they might help you comprehend who you are.

Finding your passion might help you concentrate on the things you are most enthusiastic about and the things you want to pursue with your life. It may also assist you in recognizing your talents and shortcomings and how to make the most of them.

Finding your passion may be a terrific method for introverts to get to know themselves and their interests. It may assist you in identifying your true passions and the ways in which you might utilize them to change the world.

Finding methods to communicate yourself and your thoughts might be made easier when you know what your passion is. Finding methods to express your passion might be a terrific approach to open up and communicate your ideas and emotions because introverts often struggle to express themselves.

Finding your passion might also assist you in establishing connections with others. Finding methods to connect with individuals who share your interest may be a terrific approach to develop relationships and receive support since introverts often find it difficult to connect with others.

Lastly, discovering your passion might help you discover methods to change the world. Introverts sometimes believe they lack the ability to influence others, however discovering methods to channel your enthusiasm may

CHAPTER 3

Exploring your true-self as an Extrovert.

Being an extrovert and discovering who you really are can be a pleasant and illuminating experience. You probably get your energy from social contact and love being around other people if you're an extrovert. Also, you could be more forceful and extroverted than introverts, and you might find it simpler to express yourself in social settings.

Knowing your talents and limitations is the first step towards discovering your actual extrovert self. Think about your personality qualities and how they impact how you interact with other people. Take into account your reactions to various circumstances and interactions with other individuals. Consider your favorite pastimes and the things that give you the most energy.

You may start to look into methods to leverage your strengths and weaknesses to your advantage after you have a better grasp of them. For instance, if you are an outgoing person who likes being around others, you may want to think about joining a group or club that enables you to socialize with new people and have deep talks. If you are an outspoken extrovert, you may want to search for chances to stand up in front of groups or take on leadership positions.

Understanding your values and beliefs is another important part of discovering your actual extrovert self. Spend some time reflecting about your values and the way you wish to spend your life. Think about the connections you want to have and the job you want to have. Think about your objectives and aspirations, and consider how your extroverted personality may assist you in achieving them.

Last but not least, discovering your actual extrovert self requires taking chances and stepping beyond of your comfort zone. Never be hesitant to take risks or put yourself in new circumstances. You will have a greater grasp of who you are and what you are capable of as a person as a result of this, which will aid in your personal growth and development.

Being an extrovert and discovering your real self may be difficult yet rewarding. You may develop a deeper awareness of who you are and how to utilize your extroverted personality to your advantage by taking the time to study your strengths and limitations, researching your values and beliefs, and stepping outside of your comfort zone.

Understanding your strength/weakness as an introvert/extrovert.

An essential component of self-awareness is realizing one's strengths and weaknesses as an introvert or extrovert. Understanding your personality type may help you communicate with others more effectively, approach things differently, and make the most of your talents and shortcomings.

Quiet, restrained, and contemplative are common stereotypes of introverts. People often choose to work alone and deliberate over choices. They may be quite imaginative and often have outstanding listening skills. They may also be incredibly detail-oriented and adept at fixing problems.

One of an introvert's talents is their capacity for in-depth contemplation and self-reflection. They might be quite analytical and are often competent at comprehending complicated ideas. Also, they often have a strong capacity for empathy and understanding of others.

Introverts' flaws include an excessive self-critical streak and a propensity for becoming easily overwhelmed. Moreover, they may be too sensitive to criticism and susceptible to discouragement. They could also be easily distracted and prone to procrastination.

Extroverts are often characterized as chatty, vivacious, and outgoing. They often favor working in teams and taking action promptly. They often excel at networking and have strong persuasion skills. They may be incredibly organized and often excel at multitasking.

Extroverts are good decision-makers because they can think rapidly and act swiftly. They often excel at networking and have strong persuasion skills. They may be incredibly organized and often excel at multitasking.

Extroverts tend to be too chatty and easily sidetracked, which are some of their shortcomings. Also, they have a tendency to be extremely competitive and quickly irritated. Also, they could have a tendency to make rash judgments and be quickly overwhelmed.

You may better understand yourself and how you connect with others by being aware of the advantages and disadvantages of both introverts and extroverts. You may make better use of your skills and shortcomings by understanding your personality type.

CHAPTER 4

Overcoming Social Anxiety

Many individuals have moments of anxiety or self-consciousness, such as while making a speech or attending a job interview. Yet social anxiety disorder, sometimes known as social phobia, goes beyond normal shyness or apprehension. An overwhelming dread of some social settings, particularly those that are new to you or where you believe you'll be observed or judged by others, is a symptom of social anxiety disorder. Some scenarios may be so terrifying that you experience anxiety simply thinking about them or take extreme measures to prevent them, which would cause chaos in your life.

The dread of being watched, criticized, or humiliated in public underlies social anxiety disorder. You can be concerned that other people will have negative opinions of you or that you won't measure up to them. Yet despite the fact that you are aware that your worries about being evaluated are at least partially unreasonable and exaggerated, you still struggle with feeling uneasy.

Those who have social anxiety disorder may not be forceful enough, be very subservient, or, less often, be very dominating in conversation. They could have an excessively stiff posture, make poor eye contact, or talk in an excessively quiet tone. Individuals with social anxiety disorder constantly and intensely dread engaging in any kind of general social engagement. They try to steer clear of social settings whenever possible since the prospect that someone would notice them or draw attention to them triggers both mental and physical symptoms.

The following situations may trigger social anxiety:

1. Meeting new people or speaking with "important" people

2. Public speaking or speaking up at a meeting

3. Any public performance situation

3. Eating or drinking in public

4. Using a public restroom

5. Being the center of attention in a social situation or being watched

The main distinction between social anxiety and "shyness" is the prevalence of dread or anxiety in social circumstances. They consistently experience the unease, trepidation, and dread of rejection. When someone with social anxiety is aware of impending social events, they may spend weeks or even months worrying about the possibility of saying or doing something humiliating.

Often, people with social anxiety disorder will make every effort to avoid a trigger. Nonetheless, if avoidance is not an option, they will take all reasonable measures to blend in. For instance, individuals can suffer silently while loitering in an empty space during a gathering or standing outside the action.

The dread that someone could see their outward signs of anxiousness adds to their mental distress. Excessive perspiration, a red face or flushing, trembling hands, and voice shakiness are all outward manifestations of their great fear and shame. They could also be feeling additional social anxiety symptoms inside, such as nausea, vertigo, a racing heart, or shortness of breath. A panic attack or anxiety attack may occur as a consequence of all these worsening anxiety symptoms, which together produce an intolerable condition of being.

Social anxiety and introversion/extroversion have a complicated connection. While introversion and extroversion are sometimes seen as being at different ends of the same spectrum, research indicates that neither one is necessarily associated with social anxiety. In actuality, extroverted or introverted personalities may both suffer from social anxiety.

Nonetheless, studies do indicate that introverts may have higher rates of social anxiety than extroverts. This may be because introverts are more inclined to overthink social situations and are more sensitive to social signals. They could also be more inclined to dwell on bad memories, which make them more prone to suffer worry.

On the other hand, since they are more extroverted, extroverts could be less prone to struggle with social anxiety. They could be more willing to take chances and feel more at ease in social settings.

Generally, the traits of extroversion or introversion are not always associated with social anxiety. Research does, however, indicate that introverts may be more prone to social anxiety than extroverts. Despite the fact that everyone is unique and social anxiety may affect anybody, regardless of personality type, it is crucial to keep this in mind.

Ways to develop new habits to help ease and overcome your social anxiety.

1. Refute your pessimistic and worried ideas. There may be instances when you feel unable to change how you feel or how you think. But, there are really a lot of things that may be helpful.

Changing your mindset and stifling negative ideas might help to lessen social anxiety symptoms. Start by recognizing the fearful ideas that come to mind when you consider social settings. Examine and question these ideas after that. Ask yourself why you think this way and whether you are really feeling this way or if you are just making a habit of presuming the worse. While it takes time and there is no quick remedy, it is possible to alter your way of thinking since the mind is a strong tool.

2. Pay attention. You may be present and aware of your thoughts and emotions in a non-judgmental and helpful manner by practicing mindful awareness and being attentive. It has been discovered that meditation affects the activity of some brain regions. Four 20-minute mindfulness meditation sessions were offered to participants with average levels of anxiety. After mindfulness training, they discovered that anxiety levels might drop by up to 39%.

3. Visit a coffee house. Try bringing your tablet or laptop to the closest coffee shop

if you want to watch movies online or catch up on your favorite TV program. Do something you like and are comfortable with in a situation that would otherwise make you nervous. You will be pushing your limits while enjoying the familiarity and comfort of being able to focus only on what you're doing. Ideally, you can exert some mental effort while yet maintaining your comfort level.

4. Establish a hierarchy for exposure. Describe and rank your level of anxiety in each social circumstance. For instance, a score of 0 indicates little anxiety while a score of 10 indicates a severe panic episode.

Create a list and note your feelings for each circumstance, no matter how trivial or significant. Asking a stranger on the subway for the time entering a room during an event. It's crucial to record your forecasts on paper so that you can recall them when the time comes to really go through them.

5. Avoid concentrating on yourself. When you're in circumstances that especially make you uneasy, it might be difficult to stop the constant mental chatter. We often turn inward and concentrate on how we will come across to others, nearly usually expecting that it will be negatively. the idea that when you enter a room, everyone will be staring at you and evaluating you in some way? This is not true.

Give up worrying about who you are and what others think of you. Make an effort to be present, keep others in mind, and establish genuine relationships. Try to be present and pay attention to what is being said; nobody is perfect.

6. Change your lifestyle for the better to lessen anxiety. Since the mind and body are intertwined, how you treat your body may have a big influence on how you feel about yourself and how anxious you are. Making little lifestyle adjustments might help you feel more confident and be better able to handle the symptoms of anxiety. Prevent or reduce your caffeine intake by delaying the consumption of coffee and other caffeinated beverages. Energy drinks have a stimulating effect and might make anxiety symptoms worse.

Make it a point to be active throughout the day; even a quick stroll during your lunch break is a fantastic way to fit it in. Make physical activity a priority in your life.

Alcohol might raise your risk of having an anxiety attack even if it may seem to settle your anxieties. Get enough good sleep, remain hydrated, and drink lots of water. Lack of sleep makes you considerably more prone to anxiety and might have a negative impact on your mood. According to recent studies, sleep deprivation might really contribute to anxiety disorders.

7. Inhale and exhale. Anxiety might manifest physically as racing heart,

thumping chest, lightheadedness, and tense muscles. You may regain control of your body by learning to take a moment and calm down your breathing.

Just sit down, make yourself comfortable, and take your deepest breath of the day, holding it for four seconds. After then, gently exhale while exhaling as much air as you can. After you feel your breath beginning to calm down to its regular rhythm, take another deep inhale, filling your stomach with air.

8. Display confidence. Adults who have severe shyness and social anxiety are in great numbers. The same way you learned to ride a bike, you may learn to be more self-assured. Act with greater

assurance, and people will respond favorably.

You don't have to be the popular kid or the focus of attention as a result. Simply said, you need to be more forceful. Initially alarming things will start to feel better with time.

9. Look for social settings and participate. Make an attempt to interact with others more. Actively seek out social settings that may benefit you in overcoming your phobias. Maybe start with a lesson on social skills. Before entering the real world, you may properly practice social interactions here. This will provide you with some advice on what to say and do in social situations that you are unsure about or concerned about.

10. Show yourself some love. Everyone has feelings of embarrassment at some time in their lives since nobody is flawless. The struggle to overcome social anxiety is real. There may be instances when you think negatively and revert to old patterns. It's possible to feel more nervous than usual if you're exhausted or worn down, but it doesn't indicate you've failed. Just take a moment to breathe in the moment and put the strategies you've been working on into practice.

11. Talk. By conquering shyness and social anxiety, you should start to feel more at ease in social situations. Knowing what to say while talking to someone may be really difficult. An uncomfortable pause

might sometimes seem to go on forever. You may progressively reduce your anxiety by approaching individuals.

12. Defeat your phobias. Face your worries as the last step. If you don't put yourself in circumstances where you feel uncomfortable, you will never be able to conquer social anxiety. You won't be doing yourself any favors or promoting personal development if you use avoidance as a coping mechanism.

Exposure therapy, or confronting your anxieties, has been shown to be useful in treating anxiety disorders in several studies. Nonetheless, research does indicate that exposure should be used sparingly. So start small and work your way up by engaging in social interactions or activities that just slightly make you anxious.

The road to recovery from social anxiety is arduous, and it takes time for new brain connections necessary for social engagement to emerge. Is your everyday life consistently impacted by social anxiety? Therefore don't be afraid to search for expert assistance in whichever way you feel comfortable doing so. These are excellent strategies for overcoming social anxiety. Even if it seems like an insurmountable challenge, it's so worth conquering so you may fully enjoy your life.

CHAPTER 5

Developing Your Extroverted Side

Extroverts get their energy from interacting with others. Extroverts often experience excitement while socializing with others. They tend to have strong self-esteem in general and a lot of social confidence. They are often characterized by others as chatty, gregarious, and friendly.

Extroverts are also more inclined to take risks, particularly those involving their health.

The following are a few general traits linked to extroversion:

1. Takes pleasure in being the focus of attention

2. Like working in groups

3. feels lonely when spending too much time alone

4. Enjoys chatting to others

5. Enjoys discussing emotions and opinions

6. Seek ideas and inspiration from other people and other sources.

7. Many, varied interests

8. Often takes action before considering.

The development of an extrovert side for an introvert can be a difficult process, but it is possible. It requires a commitment to self-exploration and a willingness to take risks.

The first step in developing an extrovert side is to identify the introvert's strengths and weaknesses. Introverts tend to be more reflective and thoughtful, but they may also be more prone to overthinking and rumination. It is important to recognize these tendencies and use them to one's advantage. For example, an introvert may be able to think through a problem more thoroughly than an extrovert, but they may need to take more time to do so.

Introverts have much strength that can help in the development of an extrovert side. For example, introverts are often good listeners, which can help them to better understand the needs and perspectives of others. They are also often more thoughtful and reflective, which can help them to think through decisions and come up with creative solutions. Additionally, introverts are often more independent and self-reliant, which can help them to take initiative and be more assertive.

On the other hand, introverts can also have weaknesses that can hinder the development of an extrovert side. For example, introverts may be more prone to overthinking and ruminating, which can lead to indecision and inaction. Additionally, introverts may be more prone to shyness and social anxiety, which can make it difficult to take risks and be more outgoing.

However, introverts can use their strengths and weaknesses to help develop their extrovert side. For example, introverts can use their listening skills to better understand the needs and perspectives of others, which can help them to be more empathetic and open-minded. They can also use their independent and self-reliant nature to take initiative and be more assertive. Additionally, introverts can use their tendency to overthink and ruminate to think through decisions and come up with creative solutions. Finally, introverts can use their shyness and social anxiety to practice taking risks and being more outgoing in small, safe environments.

Another step is to practice being more outgoing. This can be done in small steps, such as introducing oneself to new people, joining a club or organization, or attending social events. It is important to remember that it is okay to be uncomfortable in these situations, and that it is normal to feel anxious or overwhelmed. It is also important to remember that it is okay to make mistakes and that it is part of the learning process.

Being more outgoing can help in the development of an extrovert side in many ways. Practical examples of how to be more outgoing include:

1. Participating in group activities: Joining a club or group activity can help to build confidence and social skills. This could be anything from a sports team to a book club. Being part of a group can help to build relationships and create a sense of belonging.

2. Making conversation: Making conversation with strangers can be intimidating, but it is a great way to practice being more outgoing. Start small by introducing yourself to someone in line at the grocery store or striking up a conversation with a classmate.

3. Volunteering: Volunteering is a great way to meet new people and practice being more outgoing. It can also be a great way to give back to the community and make a difference.

4. Taking risks: Taking risks can be scary, but it can also be a great way to practice being more outgoing. This could be anything from trying a new activity to speaking up in a meeting. Taking risks can help to build confidence and help to develop an extrovert side.

5. Social media: Social media can be a great way to practice being more outgoing. It can be a great way to connect with people from all over the world and practice making conversation.

The third step is to take care of yourself. This involves getting adequate rest, eating well, and taking part in enjoyable and relaxing activities. It's also crucial to speak to oneself positively and to constantly remind oneself that it's normal to be an introvert.

Self-care is a crucial component in discovering your extroverted side. Self-care may make you more extroverted, self-assured, and at ease in social circumstances. Here are some helpful advices on taking care of yourself to help you become more outgoing:

1. Get adequate sleep. Both physical and mental health depends on getting enough sleep. Make sure you get enough sleep every night so you have the strength and concentration to be more outgoing.

2. Regular exercise may improve your mood and make you more outgoing since it produces endorphins.

3. Consume a nutritious diet: A good diet may improve your mood and provide you the energy you need to be more outgoing.

4. Hang out with pals: Having friends around might make you feel more at ease and connected in social settings.

5. Take some time to unwind and recharge: Be sure to give yourself some alone time. You may become more self-assured and equipped to handle social settings as a result.

6. Talk to yourself positively. Positive self-talk may make you feel more certain and prepared to handle social settings.

7. Take risks: Taking chances might make you more outgoing. Go outside of your comfort zone or try something new.

8. Develop mindfulness: Mindfulness may assist you in being attentive and present in social settings.

You may improve your self-confidence, outgoingness, and social comfort by taking care of yourself. This may encourage you to become more outgoing and make it simpler for you to accept difficulties.

The fourth phase involves assertiveness training. This entails standing up for oneself and outlining one's requirements and desires. It's important to keep in mind that setting limits and saying "no" are acceptable behaviors.

By training people how to communicate their views and emotions in a confident and straightforward way, practicing assertiveness may aid in the development of an extrovert side. Being assertive is having the capacity to communicate one's ideas and emotions in an open, straightforward, and non-aggressive manner. It is a skill that can be picked up and improved with practice.

Here are some doable actions to assist you in developing your assertiveness and extrovert qualities:

1. Recognize your sentiments. Before you can assertively express yourself, it's critical to recognize and comprehend your feelings. Spend some time considering your feelings and the reasons behind them.

2. Develop self-awareness: An essential component of assertiveness is being aware of your own ideas and emotions. Be aware of how you are interacting with other people and pay attention to your body language and facial emotions.

3. Express yourself: After recognizing your emotions and developing self-awareness, it's time to speak out. While speaking to people, be assertive and straightforward. To communicate your ideas and emotions

in a direct and succinct way, use "I" sentences.

4. Listen and be receptive to criticism: Being assertive involves more than simply expressing oneself; it also involves paying attention to others. Be receptive to criticism and prepared to make concessions if needed.

5. Practice: It takes time and effort to become an assertive person. Make an attempt to be more aggressive in your daily interactions.

You may become more outgoing by learning to express one-self directly and boldly via the practice of assertiveness. You may practice being more open to new experiences and more at ease in social settings.

The fifth step is to practice self-compassion. This means being kind and understanding to oneself, even when mistakes are made. It is important to remember that everyone makes mistakes and that it is okay to make mistakes.

Practicing self-compassion can help in the development of an extrovert side by allowing individuals to be more open and accepting of themselves. Self-compassion involves treating oneself with kindness and understanding, even when faced with difficult emotions or situations. Here are some practical steps to help develop an extrovert side through self-compassion:

1. Acknowledge your feelings: Take a few moments to recognize and accept your

feelings without judgment. This can help you to be more open to new experiences and to be more comfortable in social situations.

2. Talk to yourself: Talk to yourself in a kind and understanding way. Remind yourself that it is okay to make mistakes and that you are capable of learning and growing.

3. Practice mindfulness: Mindfulness can help you to be more aware of your thoughts and feelings in the present moment. This can help you to be more open to new experiences and to be more comfortable in social situations.

4. Take risks: Taking risks can help you to become more extroverted. Try something new or step out of your comfort zone.

This can help you to become more confident and open to new experiences.

5. Connect with others: Connecting with others can help you to become more extroverted. Reach out to friends and family or join a club or organization. This can help you to become more comfortable in social situations and to be more open to new experiences.

6. Celebrate your successes: Celebrate your successes, no matter how small. This can help you to become more confident and to be more open to new experiences.

By practicing self-compassion, individuals can become more open and accepting of themselves and more comfortable in social situations. This can help them to become more extroverted and to be more open to new experiences.

Finally, it is important to remember that developing an extrovert side is a process and that it takes time. It is important to be patient and to recognize that progress may be slow. It is also important to remember that it is okay to take breaks and to give oneself time to rest and recharge.

CHAPER 6

Finding Balance

Understanding and respecting the distinctions between an introvert and an extrovert is crucial to finding a balance between the two. Creating a setting that suits both personalities is crucial as well. For instance, an extrovert may want more social engagement to feel invigorated whereas an introvert may require more alone time to recuperate.

It's also critical to understand and be ready to accommodate the demands of both personas. An extrovert may need to be more accepting of an introvert's need for alone time, while an introvert may need to be more receptive to social activities.

The neurotransmitter dopamine, a feel-good hormone secreted by the brain, is the primary distinction between an introvert's brain and an extrovert's brain. A research discovered that incentives like food, sex, social engagement, and financial success cause the brain of the extrovert to produce more dopamine, the feel-good chemical. Extroverts create vivid, uplifting recollections of the action. Contrarily, introverts have a smaller dopamine increase and are thus less likely to link the activity with pleasure. In other words, everyone interprets the same event in their own unique manner. Extroverts value social interaction with others far more than introverts do.

The depth and awareness of their inner world their thoughts, emotions, ideas, and imagination are introverts' greatest assets. They may succeed in fields like design, science, the arts, and composing stories, among others. They may spend hours alone without losing out on social engagement since they are highly at ease in their own personal zone. They are in touch with themselves and need less stimulation from the outside world. Their communication is restricted yet in-depth, and so are their character and range of interests.

On the other hand, the weakness of introverts is their emotional aversion to other people due to their obsession with their own world. They could come out as pathologically shy or socially distant as a result of this. Their confidence may be damaged if they are evaluated by others from the outside world. Due to this, they may not be able to fully use their own powers. Also, it negatively impacts their relationships and social lives.

Extroverts are good at interacting with others and making others laugh. They put a greater emphasis on interpersonal skills and are good in jobs like advertising, journalism, education, sales, and marketing that involve working with people. They can interact with strangers since they feel at ease with others. Extroverts have a wide range of interests and a wide number of subjects, and they communicate pretty effectively.

On the downside, they might be disconnected from their own internal world and need continual human engagement. They could struggle in private, peaceful times since they want company all the time. Extroverts may not be affected by this since they can still enchant others; nevertheless, it may have a negative impact on their personal relationships and self-awareness.

Few tips that can help introverts and extroverts accept themselves and find the right balance within themselves as well as their surroundings

1. Social awareness of introversion and extroversion

2. Recognizing one's own personality attribute, such as extroversion or introversion, and using it as a springboard for finding balance.

3. Although while extroverts often get their inspiration and vitality from their surroundings, they must realize that they don't always need to be charming and the life of the party. They can communicate through their feelings and personalities while allowing some opportunity for contemplation.

4. Introverts understand that being quiet while observing others is a kind of socializing. They are not required to experience the strain of required group involvement. Also, they can relate to others thanks to their creativity and originality.

5. Family members and friends would have to understand that introverts often take a while to warm up to people in social circumstances and require time to open up.

6. Extroverts' loved ones and friends must understand that they must be patient when they express their deepest emotions.

In conclusion, it is important to remember that embracing your true self is a journey that requires patience and dedication. It is not something that can be achieved overnight, but with the right attitude and the right tools, you can become an extrovert and enjoy the benefits that come with it. From an Introvert to an Extrovert: A Guide to

Embracing Your True Self has provided you with the necessary information and guidance to help you on your journey. So, take the first step and start embracing your true self today!

Good luck!